Dips

Dip cookbook for dip recipes from easy dips to party dips

Elisabetta Parisi

© 2012 by *Elisabetta Parisi*

All Rights Reserved. No part of this publication may be reproduced in any form or by any means, including scanning, photocopying, or otherwise without prior written permission of the copyright holder.

Disclaimer and Terms of Use: The Author and Publisher has strived to be as accurate and complete as possible in the creation of this book, notwithstanding the fact that she does not warrant or represent at any time that the contents within are accurate due to the rapidly changing nature of science and medicine. While all attempts have been made to verify information provided in this publication, the Author and Publisher assumes no responsibility for errors, omissions, or contrary interpretation of the subject matter herein. Any perceived slights of specific persons, peoples, or organizations are unintentional. In practical advice books, like anything else in life, there are no guarantees of any results obtained. Readers are cautioned to rely on their own judgment and seek professional medical advice about their individual circumstances and to act accordingly.

First Printing, 2012

ISBN - 13: 978-1481179515

ISBN - 10: 1481179519

Printed in the United States of America

Dedication

To all experimenters

Dips

Table of Contents

Introduction 9
Easy Dip Recipes 13
    Creamy garlic and herb 14
    Creamy smoked salmon 16
    Ginger dip 17
    Greek style cream dip 20
    Roasted red pepper dip 21
    Mustard and honey dip 22
    Humus variations 24
    Tomato and cherry pepper dip 27
    Cheese curry dip 28
    Beetroot Meze style dip 30
    Spinach cream dip 31
    Shrimp and Cheddar dip 32
    Lobster dip 33
    Parmesan and Mozzarella 35
    Cream cheese and radish dip 37
    Cheesy Mexican corn and black bean dip 40
    Feta cheese and garlic dip 42
    Peanut butter dip 45
    Green cheese dip 46
    Bread oil dip 47
    Guacamole 49
    Crunchy nut fruit dip 50
    Creamy fruit dip 52
More Difficult Dip Recipes 53
    Pepperoni and cream cheese dip 54
    Yogurt and toasted cumin dip 55
    Blue cheese and shallot dip 56
    Hot Cheddar dip 57

- Cheesy beer dip 58
- Bacon and tomato dip 59
- Caramelized onion dip 60
- Cheddar Fondue 62
- Mushroom dip 64
- Thai style dip 65
- Beef chilli cheese dip 66
- Chicken Enchilada Dip 67
- Mexican style hot bean dip 69
- Crab and spinach dip 71
- Baked spinach and artichoke Dip 72
- Clam and cheese dip 74
- Mexican style layer dip 75

Conclusion 77
About the Author 79

Introduction

Dips tend to be the things that you pick up last minute, without much thought and a resignation that you will end up with the same old worn out recipes that supermarkets love to specialize in. You will take them home and often only eat a little of each with the rest left to go off in the refrigerator. It doesn't have to be like this. You can make your own dips. There are lots of different recipes that you can customize and make into your own specialities. With these dips you will be lucky to have enough to last the night. Sometimes I have made a dip for guests and ended up eating it before they arrive! This means that another batch has to be put together really quickly, but what the heck food is to be enjoyed, right?

Dips can make a snack or an appetizer. If you take a dip to parties you know that you have a winner when it quickly disappears and people keep asking you for the recipe. This can be fun in itself. It is also fun making a variation on a dip and then trying it out on your family and friends. Needless to say, some will be keepers and others won't. Despite failures there is always a need to try different things out. This may simply be due to wondering what will happen to the dip if you add a particular ingredient or maybe increase or decrease the amounts of it in a recipe. What ever you do, you will be creating something new. I guess what I am trying to say is that it is ok to experiment and that you don't have to slavishly follow the recipes that are given here in this book.

Variations are suggested for most of the recipes where they are appropriate. This can help if you haven't got the particular ingredient at the time. You can therefore use substitutions to give interesting different dips on the same basic theme.

A lot of people are interested in reducing the fat content of their dips. The main recipes given here use the standard ingredients rather than reduced fat ones. It is possible to substitute low fat soft cheese, sour cream or yogurt in the recipes but you have to consider the effect that it may have on the thickness of your dips. If you are happy with a runnier dip then it is not a problem at all. However, if you want to maintain the thickness you may have to consider adding thickening agents to the recipes as well. This may include corn starch and gelatine type products.

You may find that the quantities given in the list of ingredients may produce too much of the dip for your needs. As a result you may need to adjust the amounts to give the portion size that you want. I do this all of the time as I am often making a dip just for myself as part of a tasty snack while I am at home watching the TV. It can be useful to know some equivalents in measurements to make it easier to work out the amounts you need. An example of this is where you are asked to use a quarter of a cup of a particular ingredient. If you want to reduce this to a quarter of the amount you would be trying to judge 1/8 of a cup. This would be difficult to do. It would therefore be a lot easier to convert the measurements to something smaller such as tablespoons. Here are some useful equivalents.

1 oz = 2 tbsp
1 cup = 16 tbsp
3 tsp = 1 tbsp

When reducing the quantities in the dip recipes you need to bear in mind that that if a blender is to be used there needs to be enough material to allow the blades to pick up the ingredients and actually cut them up. With only small amounts in the blender this won't happen.

You can also make estimates of the amounts that you need by looking at the relative amounts of each ingredient. In a recipe that has 200g of cream cheese and 100g of yogurt then it is clear that you need twice as much of the cream cheese compared to the yogurt. This is very useful when you are trying to put together a dip in the last few minutes before guests arrive or just can't be bothered to do all of the measuring.

A lot of dips improve over time when they are chilled in a refrigerator. As a result it is a good idea to try and prepare your dips the day before you need them. This way they can develop their flavour as they chill over night.

All of the recipes listed in the 'Easy Dip Recipes' section only require that the ingredients are mixed in some way whether that involves stirring, blending or putting into a food processor. There will be no cooking involved at all. In the 'More Difficult Dip Recipes' section you may have to fry or cook some of the ingredients as part of the dip preparation as well as doing mixing and blending as well. Some dips in this section may also require the baking of the dip in an oven.

Easy Dip Recipes

These dips can easily be prepared with often just a few ingredients and some degree of mixing or blending.

Creamy garlic and herb

This is an amazing cream dip, which is both tasty and very easy to make. This is a mild dip and therefore ideal for serving up to children and teenagers.

Creamy garlic and herb with fresh dill and fresh basil

Ingredients

100g soft cheese
50g yogurt
1 garlic clove
1 handful of chives
Lemon juice
Freshly ground black pepper

Method

Mix the soft cheese with the low fat yoghurt. This is easier if the cream cheese is softened. You can do this by putting it in the microwave for a few seconds before mixing it with the yogurt. Be careful not to over heat it.

Crush the garlic clove and snip the chives into short lengths. Stir these into the cheese and yoghurt mixture. Add a little lemon juice and fresh ground black pepper to taste. Mix these into the dip and serve with cheese sticks and plain tortilla chips or crackers.

Try using other fresh herbs such as basil and dill.

Creamy smoked salmon

This is an easy to make tasty cream style dip which is also low in fat.

Ingredients

100g light soft cheese
50g low fat yogurt
125g smoked salmon
A few sprigs of dill

Method

Mix the soft cheese with the low fat yoghurt

Chop the smoked salmon and then chop the dill. Mix these 2 ingredients together and then stir into the soft cheese and yogurt mixture.

Try adding basil or mint instead of the dill or as well as.

Ginger dip

Ginger dip directly after blending

Ingredients

1 onion
1 inch fresh ginger
¼ cup fresh lemon juice
½ cup white vinegar
½ cup soy sauce

Method

Peel the ginger and then use a cheese grater so that any fibrous texture from the ginger root is removed. Chop the onion.

Use the medium to small grater to reduce the root fibres

Place the ginger, onion, lemon juice, vinegar and soy sauce into a blender and use the pulse feature until all of the ingredients are well blended.

If you aren't sure about the amount of soy sauce that you want in the dip you should start with a 1/3 of a cup and then gradually add extra to the mixture in the blender until you get it to your liking.

Low sodium soy sauce can be used if it is preferred. A slightly different taste is achieved by using rice vinegar or wine vinegar instead of the white vinegar. This dip goes very well with fish dippers such as prawns or salmon. It is also good with chicken such as skewers or nuggets. Try it with raw vegetables and pieces of steak as well.

Greek style cream dip

A very simple low fat dip to make that is ideal to serve with pita chips. As well as using this as a dip you can also serve it as a sauce with chicken skewers for a tasty treat.

Ingredients

100g light soft cheese
50g low fat yogurt
Half a cucumber
Handful of mint leaves

Method

Mix the soft cheese with the low fat yoghurt

Grate the cucumber and chop the mint leaves. Add these to the cheese and yoghurt and make sure that they are mixed in well before serving.

Roasted red pepper dip

Ingredients

7 oz jar roasted red peppers
½ cup cream cheese
2 green onions
1 clove garlic
1 tbsp lemon juice
Dill

Method

Drain the liquids off the peppers and then rinse them in cold water and drain once again. Coarsely chop the green onions and the garlic.

Put the red peppers, cream cheese, green onions, garlic, and lemon juice into a blender and make sure that it is pureed into a nice smooth consistency.

Put the dip into a serving dish, cover and then chill in the refrigerator for a few hours until it has set. Sprinkle dill on the top and then serve with a selection of yellow bell pepper, small white button mushrooms, carrot sticks, celery sticks and courgette sticks. It also goes well with crackers or focaccia bread.

You can give this dip a bit of a kick by adding some hot pepper sauce or red pepper flakes. You can easily change its nature by adding other ingredients for example crab meat.

Mustard and honey dip

Mustard and honey dip with cheese crackers

Ingredients

½ cup mayonnaise
¼ cup mustard
¼ cup honey
1 dash salt
Cayenne pepper

Method

Put the mayonnaise, mustard and honey into a mixing bowl. Stir and combine the ingredients. Add salt and cayenne seasoning to taste and continue to stir the dip until it is smooth. Cover the bowl and put it into the refrigerator to chill before serving with chicken fingers, popcorn chicken, chicken nuggets, chicken tenders, pretzel sticks or fries.

Using whole grain mustard adds an extra dimension to this recipe which makes it ideal for dipping with prawns. For a bit of extra kick use spicy Dijon mustard or increase the cayenne content up to 1 tsp.

Humus variations

You can easily make your own homemade humus dips using this simple recipe. With a recipe this simple and tasty you won't want to go back to shop bought humus ever again.

Humus with coriander

Ingredients

400g can chickpeas
1 tbsp tahini paste
1 large garlic clove
3 tbsp Greek style yogurt
Lemon juice
Salt and pepper

Method

Chop the large garlic clove. You need both the chickpeas and the liquid from the can of chickpeas so open the can and drain the liquid through a sieve into a small bowl.

Put the yogurt, chickpeas, tahini and chopped garlic into a blender. Blend the mixture until it is really smooth. At this point the humus will be really thick so add a little of the saved chickpea liquid and blend again. Only add a little of the liquid at a time or otherwise the humus will become too sloppy. Repeat until you have the desired thickness. Pour and spoon the mixture into a bowl and then stir in lemon juice and seasoning to get the taste that you want.

You can leave out the tahini and still get good tasting humus. Half a teaspoon of cumin powder can also act as a substitute for the flavour of the tahini if you haven't got it to hand.

You can also experiment with adding other ingredients such as fresh coriander leaves, cumin, paprika, roasted red peppers or ground chilli. If you find that the humus is a little bitter then you should consider cutting back on the amount of tahini paste. You can also substitute lime for lemon which will give the recipe an extra dimension.

If you find getting the tahini paste a difficulty you can make your own by blending 3 parts sesame seeds with 1 part olive oil. As well as being homemade it can also cut down the cost of buying the tahini paste.

You can make a spicy harissa topping for the humus by mixing 2 tbsp of harissa paste with 1 tbsp of tomato puree.

You can also prepare your own chickpeas from uncooked ones. This does take a lot longer to do but home prepared chickpeas tend to be a lot softer than the canned ones and as a result they can end up making a more buttery and smooth humus.

To prepare your own chickpeas you should first put 200g of the uncooked chickpeas in a bowl. Next add twice the volume of cold water to cover them. Mix in 1 teaspoon of bicarbonate of soda and then leave the chickpeas to soak for 24 hours. After this time, drain the water from the chickpeas and rinse them well in cold water. Add the chickpeas to a large saucepan and add ½ a teaspoon of bicarbonate of soda. Cover the pan and then heat until boiling. Reduce the heat and simmer for between 1 and 2 hours. If the water level drops add more boiling water to the pan during cooking. After cooking leave the pan to cool and then drain the chickpeas well making sure that you save the cooking water from the pan for use later. These cooked chickpeas can be used in the humus recipe in the same way as the canned ones and the cooking water used as before to get the right consistency for the humus. If you prepare a lot of cooked chickpeas you can freeze them in portions for use in later humus recipes.

Tomato and cherry pepper dip

Ingredients

Jar of pickled sweet cherry peppers
3 tomatoes
1 tbsp sundried tomato paste
Bunch of chives
Freshly ground black pepper

Method

Roughly chop the tomatoes and snip the chives up into short lengths. Drain the jar of cherry peppers and put the peppers into a blender. Next add the chopped tomatoes, tomato paste and the majority of the snipped chives.

Blend the mixture together for a short time so that it is still made up of chunks. Add pepper seasoning to taste and poor the dip into a serving dish. Sprinkle the rest of the snipped chives on the top and serve with such things as raw vegetable sticks and tortilla crisps.

You can substitute a jar of roasted red peppers for the cherry peppers if you need to. Roasted peppers are often easier to obtain and will work just as well in this dip.

You can also try substituting fresh basil or parsley for the chives in order to get variations in flavour.

Cheese curry dip

Ingredients

4 oz feta cheese
4 oz cream cheese
½ cup cottage cheese
¼ cup mayonnaise
2 garlic cloves
½ tsp curry powder
¼ tsp oregano
¼ tsp thyme
¼ tsp basil
¼ tsp dill weed
Freshly ground black pepper

Method

Soften the cream cheese by putting it in the microwave for a few seconds. Mince the garlic cloves.

Put the feta cheese, cream cheese, cottage cheese, mayonnaise, garlic, curry, oregano, thyme, basil and dill into a food processor and blend until you have a smooth mixture. Season to taste with the freshly ground black pepper

Transfer the dip into a serving bowl. Cover the bowl and place in the refrigerator to chill for a few hours. Serve with vegetable dippers or crackers.

You should adjust the amount of garlic and curry powder in the dip depending on your individual taste.

If the dip is a little too thick you can add a couple of tablespoons of milk to thin it down a little.

For a hotter dip add a few slices of pickled Jalapenos.

Beetroot Meze style dip

This is a bright and colourful dip similar to the sort served in Turkish Meze dishes.

Ingredients

250g cooked beetroot
1 garlic clove
Greek yogurt
Salt and pepper
Olive oil

Method

Peel the beetroot and crush the garlic clove. Put these into a blender or food processor and blend until a puree is formed. Add enough of the yogurt to produce a smooth dip with the right consistency. Season the dip with salt and pepper to taste and then drizzle on olive oil before serving with toasted pita bread.

Spinach cream dip

Ingredients

1 cup cottage cheese
10 oz frozen chopped spinach
1 cup sour cream
2 tbsp milk
1 tbsp grated Parmesan cheese
1 tbsp ranch salad dressing
1 tbsp teaspoon dried Dill
1 tsp dried parsley
2 tsp garlic powder
Freshly ground black pepper

Method

Thaw the spinach and then squeeze it dry.

Put the cottage cheese into a food processor and whizz it up until it is smooth. Spoon the processed cottage cheese into a bowl and then stir in the spinach, sour cream, milk, Parmesan cheese, ranch dressing, dill, parsley, and garlic powder.

Add the freshly ground black pepper to taste. Cover the bowl and put it in the refrigerator to chill for at least 3 hours. This dip goes very well with raw vegetables for dipping.

Shrimp and Cheddar dip

Ingredients

½ pound cooked shrimp
¼ cup mayonnaise
2 green onions
1 cup shredded Cheddar cheese
¼ teaspoon hot pepper sauce

Method

Finely chop the cooked shrimp and mince the onions.

Put the chopped shrimp, mayonnaise, minced onion, shredded cheese and the hot pepper sauce into a mixing bowl. Combine the ingredients together well and then cover the bowl. Put the bowl into the refrigerator to chill before serving.

Lobster dip

This dip is ideal for special occasions and it is sure to go really quickly.

Ingredients

7 oz lobster meat
1 tbsp minced onion
1 tbsp lemon juice
8 oz softened cream cheese
4 tbsp softened butter
1 tablespoon horseradish sauce

Method

You can use freshly cooked lobster meat or the canned version.

Flake the lobster meat and then put it into a mixing bowl. Add the minced onion, lemon juice, cream cheese, butter and horseradish sauce. Mix all of the ingredients in the bowl together until they have a smooth consistency. Cover the bowl and place it in the refrigerator to chill for about 30 minutes before serving.

Be careful with the amount of horseradish sauce that you add. If you aren't sure about how much you like it then add less. It is far easier to add more later on if you think it needs it rather than spoiling the dip with too much at the start.

You can make this dip the day before and keep it in the refrigerator until you need it. Be aware that the longer you leave it to stand in the refrigerator the stronger that the flavours develop. For extra flavour you can also add a minced clove of garlic to the mixture.

Parmesan and Mozzarella

This dip is excellent with raw vegetables and great way to get kids to actually have their 5 a day. It is also good when served with pretzel sticks.

Parmesan and Mozzarella with carrot sticks

Ingredients

2 cups mayonnaise
1 cup sour cream
1 cup shredded mozzarella cheese
2 tbsp grated Parmesan cheese
1 tbsp minced onion
1 tsp white sugar

1 pinch garlic salt
1 pinch seasoning salt

Method

Put the mayonnaise, mozzarella, sour cream, Parmesan, sugar, onion, garlic salt and seasoning salt into a mixing bowl and combine them together well.

Once the ingredients are well mixed cover the bowl and place it in the refrigerator for an hour to chill before serving. The longer that you leave it in the refrigerator, the more that the flavours will develop.

You could add a clove of minced garlic to the recipe if you prefer dips with greater garlic content.

Cream cheese and radish dip

This is a great way to use fresh radishes from the garden. The fresher the radishes the more flavour that they have. Everybody has a different idea about how much flavour that they want in a dip but this is simple to achieve by adjusting the amount of radish and garlic that you use.

Radish dip with crackers

Ingredients

4 cloves garlic
6-12 radishes
16oz cream cheese
Salt and pepper

Method

Peel the garlic cloves and cut each radish into quarters. Microwave the cream cheese for 15 seconds in order to soften it.

Radishes cut into quarters

Use a food processor or blender to finely mince the garlic using the machine's pulse feature. Add the minced garlic to the radishes and then mix in the cream cheese until it is blended together well. Season the dip with salt and pepper to taste. Put the dip into a dish and cover before placing it in the refrigerator to chill for an hour before you serve it with crackers or vegetables.

If you think that there isn't enough radish flavour then you can add extra or even double the amount until you get a taste that you like.

For extra flavour add 2 tbsp of chopped fresh mint to the recipe. Try not to use light cream cheese otherwise the dip may end up too runny.

Another version of this recipe can be made by using sour cream instead of the cream cheese and then adding dill weed to the recipe as well. This dip isn't quite as thick as the original but has a superb taste.

Cheesy Mexican corn and black bean dip

This is a nice light and refreshing dip with a little bit of Mexican bite. It is an exciting dip whether it is served warm or cold.

Ingredients

Two 11 oz cans Mexican style corn
15 oz can black beans
1 cup mayonnaise
2 cups sour cream
1 bunch green onions
½ cup chopped fresh coriander leaves
1 pound shredded Cheddar cheese
1 teaspoon fresh lime juice
1 teaspoon ground cumin
Cayenne pepper to taste
1 pinch salt

Method

Open and drain the liquid from the contents of the corn and black bean cans. Chop the green onions.

Put the corn, black beans, mayonnaise, sour cream, chopped green onions, coriander leaves, cheddar cheese and lime juice into a mixing bowl and stir to combine them together well.

Season the dip with the cumin and salt and add the desired amount of cayenne pepper. It is best to start with a pinch and then decide if more is needed.

Stir the dip to blend in the seasoning and then cover the bowl and place it in the refrigerator to chill before serving. This dip goes well with tortilla chips.

An extra dimension can be achieved with this dip by baking it at 180C in the oven for about 20 minutes until it gets nice and bubbly.

Feta cheese and garlic dip

Feta and garlic dip with crackers

Ingredients

4 oz crumbled feta cheese
4 oz cream cheese
1/3 cup mayonnaise
1 minced garlic clove
¼ tsp dried basil
¼ tsp dried oregano
1/8 tsp dill weed
1/8 tsp dried thyme

Method

Soften the cream cheese by putting it in the microwave for a few seconds. Put the softened cream cheese into a mixing bowl and then add the feta cheese, mayonnaise, garlic, basil, oregano, dill and thyme. Use a hand mixer or blender to make sure that all the ingredients are well blended and a smooth dip is made. If you reduce the measurements used in this recipe you may not have enough to allow the hand blender to do its job and as a result it would be better to do the mixing by hand.

Once all of the ingredients have been mixed cover the bowl and put it in the refrigerator to chill until you are ready to serve it with vegetables and crackers or pita chips. The longer you leave it to chill the more that the flavour will develop.

Using a hand mixer to prepare the dip

Peanut butter dip

Ingredients

¼ cup peanut butter
3 cloves minced garlic
¼ cup brown sugar
¼ cup light coconut milk
¼ cup soy sauce
2 tbsp fresh lemon juice

Method

Put the peanut butter, minced garlic, brown sugar, coconut milk, soy sauce and lemon juice into a mixing bowl. Stir the ingredients until they are combined into a dip with a smooth consistency. Cover the bowl and put into the refrigerator for at least 2 hours before serving.

Some people may find the soy sauce a little over powering and as a result reducing the amount of this is a serious option. Soy sauce tends to be quite salty so reducing the amount of it will also reduce the salt content of the dip. Reducing the soy sauce may also make it more inviting for children because the peanut butter flavour will be more prominent.

This is a nice dipping sauce to use with raw vegetables such as celery, carrot sticks, red peppers and sugar snap peas. It also works well with breaded chicken strips and chicken nuggets. Due to its Asian style it also goes well with Chinese spring rolls and chicken satay.

Green cheese dip

Ingredients

5 oz feta cheese
2 tbsp extra virgin olive oil
2 tsp basil pesto

Method

Put the pesto and olive oil into a bowl and mix them together. Crumble the feta cheese and then put it into a serving bowl. Pour the pesto and oil mix over the feta cheese. Gently stir the mixture until the feta is covered in the oil and pesto mix.

Cover the dish and place it in the refrigerator to chill before serving with Tostitos, raw carrot, zucchini slices, asparagus tips, crusty bread, chips or crackers.

You can make the dip a little more interesting by adding sliced olives. Different colours can be achieved by using different kinds of pesto such as sun dried tomato pesto.

Bread oil dip

Oil dip with crusty bread

Ingredients

1 cup extra virgin olive oil
½ cup balsamic vinegar
½ cup grated parmesan cheese
1 ½ tbsp dried basil
½ teaspoon salt
½ teaspoon pepper
5 cloves garlic

Method

Mince the garlic.

Put the garlic, oil, vinegar, basil, salt, pepper and cheese in a clean jar with a secure lid. Stir the ingredients to combine them and then put the lid on the jar. Shake the mixture to blend all of the ingredients. If possible leave the dip to develop its flavour over night before using it.

Use shallow bowls to serve the dip with chunks of rustic bread for dipping into the oil.

You can adjust the amount of oil and balsamic vinegar to suit your taste. If fresh herbs are available you can chop and use them instead of the dried ones. You can also adjust the herbs depending on the ones that are available. It certainly works well with Thyme as well as oregano.

Guacamole

This is a traditional style recipe where the ingredients remain chunky. Getting the right kind of ripe avocado is central to the flavour and as a result you should use the ones that have the rough dark green skins.

Ingredients

1 large tomato
1 medium sized onion
1 green chilli
2 tbsp freshly squeezed lime juice
1 ripe California type avocado
½ tsp toasted cumin seeds
¼ cup chopped fresh coriander leaves
Salt to taste
Freshly ground black pepper to taste

Method

Dice the tomato. Finely chop the onion so that you have about 3 tablespoons. Deseed and finely chop the green chilli pepper.

Put the tomato, onion, chilli pepper and lime juice into a large bowl and combine them. Peel the avocado, remove the seed and then dice it. Add the avocado to the tomato mixture in the bowl. Stir the mixture gently so that the avocado is spread throughout. Put the toasted cumin seeds, coriander leaves, salt and pepper into the bowl and once again stir to combine the ingredients until they are well blended. Let the mixture rest for around 15 minutes so that the flavours develop and then serve with corn chips or corn tortillas for dipping.

Crunchy nut fruit dip

This is a simple recipe with a crushed nuts topping for lots of extra crunch. The nice thing about this recipe is that it is likely that you will already have the ingredients lying about in the kitchen somewhere and as a result you won't have to make a special trip to the supermarket. This also a good dip to use for kids at parties because the creamy consistency encourages them to eat more fruit instead of the overly fatty snacks they usually like.

Ingredients

16 oz cream cheese
1 cup brown sugar
2 tsp vanilla extract
Chopped nuts

Method

Soften the cream cheese by placing it in a microwave for about 15 seconds.

Place the softened cream cheese, brown sugar, and vanilla extract into a bowl and combine them using a hand mixer until it is well blended and smooth. Cover the bowl and then place it in the refrigerator for an hour to chill before sprinkling the top with the crushed nuts and serving.

This dip goes well with such fruit combinations as fruit kebabs including strawberries, grapes, pineapple, kiwis and apple. It is especially good with raspberries and blackberries. You can also serve it with ginger snaps and chocolate tortilla chips. A more adult taste can be achieved by using rum extract instead of the vanilla.

Try adding ingredients such as lemon zest, lemon juice and ginger for an extra kick.

Creamy fruit dip

This is a fantastic light and fluffy dip which can be used to go with any kinds of fruit such as melon, berries, grapes and bananas.

Ingredients

8 oz strawberry cream cheese
7 oz marshmallow creme
1 cup cool whip
2 tbsp orange juice

Method

Soften the cream cheese and then use an electric mixer to blend it with the marshmallow creme, cool whip and orange juice.

You can add 1 or 2 tsp of lemon juiced to give it a bit of extra zip. Half a tsp of vanilla extract can also add a different flavour to the dip. Adding a few drops of Maraschino cherry juice will give the dip a pink colour making it an ideal dip for combining with strawberries. You can also make a very simple dip by just using ordinary cream cheese and the marshmallow crème.

More Difficult Dip Recipes

These recipes may require you to do some cooking of the ingredients whether that be frying them or baking them in the oven. They may also contain a larger number of ingredients compared with those in the Easy Dip section.

Pepperoni and cream cheese dip

Ingredients

8 oz cream cheese
4 oz sour cream
8 oz sliced pepperoni
4 oz canned chopped green chillies

Method

Soften the cream cheese by putting it in the microwave for a few seconds. Cut the pepperoni slices into quarters.

Stir the cream cheese, sour cream, and pepperoni and chopped green chillies together in a small bowl.

Transfer the mixture to a suitable baking dish. Put the dish into a preheated oven set to 180C for about 25 minutes until the dip is heated through. Serve with Tortilla chips or wheat thins for dipping.

Instead of baking you can put all of the ingredients into a crock pot and slow cook it while stirring every now and then.

Putting slices of pepperoni on the top before baking can produce a more inviting and interesting appearance to this dip. It is ideal for parties and children seem to especially like it.

Yogurt and toasted cumin dip

Ingredients

1 small handful of fresh coriander
1 green chilli
1 tsp whole cumin seeds
500g Greek style yogurt
Extra virgin olive oil to drizzle

Method

Put the whole cumin seeds into a hot frying pan. There is no need for any oil. As they cook shake the seeds in the pan. Cook the seeds for about a minute until they turn slightly dark and you can smell the aroma from the toasting seeds. Once they are cooked tip the seeds into a mortar and when they are cool lightly crush them with a pestle. If you haven't got a pestle and mortar you can put the cooled seeds in a bag and crush them with a heavy pan or a rolling pin.

Chop the coriander leaves but keep a few intact ones for garnish. Deseed the green chilli and then chop it up.

Mix the chopped coriander, chilli and toasted cumin with the yogurt and then pour the mixture into a fine meshed sieve and suspend it over a small bowl. Allow the water to drain off the mixture for about an hour while it is chilling in the refrigerator. After this time discard the water and spoon the dip into a serving bowl. Drizzle olive oil on the top and garnish with the remaining coriander leaves immediately before serving.

Blue cheese and shallot dip

Ingredients

1 ½ cups thinly sliced shallots
1 tablespoon extra virgin olive oil
¾ cup mayonnaise
¾ cup Light Sour Cream
1 ½ cups crumbled blue cheese

Method

Put the sliced shallots into a frying pan together with the olive oil and cook them on a medium heat until they are soft. Reduce the heat to low and cook them for about a further 30 minutes or until they are golden brown in colour and caramelized. Stir the shallots every now and then as they cook. Once they are cooked allow them to cool.

Take a small bowl and put the mayonnaise and sour cream into it. Combine them together and then stir in the crumbled blue cheese and the cooked shallots. Make sure that all of the ingredients are well combined and then cover the dish and put it in the refrigerator for about 2 hours. Serve the dip with raw vegetables cut for dipping

Hot Cheddar dip

Ingredients

1 tbsp butter
1 tbsp cornstarch
¾ cup sour cream
1 cup shredded mature sharp Cheddar cheese
1 tbsp salsa

Method

Melt the butter in pan set on a medium heat. Stir in the corn starch and make sure that it is mixed in well. Next, add the sour cream and stir to combine it well. Continue heating the mixture in the pan until it is hot and bubbling nicely. At this point stir in the shredded Cheddar cheese and then the salsa. Keep stirring and heating the mixture until the cheese melts and the dip starts to thicken. Serve the dip while it is still hot

If you like your cheese sauce hot and fruity in the flavour department then you can double the amount of salsa and add some hot pepper sauce.

Cheesy beer dip

Ingredients

8 oz cream cheese
½ oz smoked Cheddar cheese
3 oz beer
¼ oz fresh baby spinach
¼ red bell pepper
1 garlic clove
2 tsp Dijon mustard
2 tsp Italian seasoning

Method

Soften the cream cheese by putting it in the microwave for a few seconds. Grate the smoked cheddar cheese. Dice the red bell pepper. Mince the garlic.

Combine the cream cheese, cheddar, beer, spinach, pepper, garlic, mustard and Italian seasoning in a mixing bowl. Mix the ingredients well and then transfer to a baking dish. Put the dish into a preheated oven set at 170C for about 20 minutes and then stir the mixture. Put the dish back in the oven and cook for a further 20 minutes. Remove from the oven and serve with toast, crostini or tortilla chips

Bacon and tomato dip

Ingredients

1 cup mayonnaise
1 cup sour cream
½ pound bacon
2 small plum tomatoes

Method

Cook the bacon well in a frying pan. Make sure that it is nice and crisp. Put the cooked bacon onto paper towels to drain and cool. Crumble the bacon into small bits. Finely chop the tomatoes.

Mix the mayonnaise, sour cream, bacon bits and chopped tomatoes together in a bowl. Make sure that the ingredients are all well combined. Cover the bowl and then put it into the refrigerator to chill for at least an hour before serving. The longer it is chilled the more that the flavour develops.

Serve with toast, assorted crackers or raw vegetables cut for dipping.

You can try adding some chopped green onions or chives for extra flavour and to make it richer try adding 4 oz of cream cheese or even grated cheddar cheese. If the bacon taste doesn't seem to be enough you can double the amount used to 1 pound.

Caramelized onion dip

Caramelized onion dip with cheese crackers

Ingredients

2 tbsp extra virgin olive oil
1 ½ cups chopped onions
¼ tsp sea salt
1 ½ cups sour cream
¾ cup mayonnaise
¼ tsp garlic powder
¼ tsp ground white pepper
½ tsp sea salt

Method

Put the onions and the oil and ¼ tsp of salt into a pan. Cook the onions on a medium heat until they are nicely browned. Make sure that the onions are well caramelized. Take the pan from the heat and put to one side to cool.

Put the sour cream, mayonnaise, garlic powder, white pepper and ½ tsp salt into a mixing bowl. Mix the ingredients until they are well combined. Stir in the cooled onions from the pan and cover the bowl. Put the bowl into the refrigerator to chill for at least an hour. The longer you chill the dip the more that the flavour develops and as a result it is sometimes a good idea to try and make it the day before you want to use it. Stir the sauce a little just before serving it with crackers or chips.

Extra onion can be added to the recipe if the onion taste isn't strong enough. This could also be caused by not chilling it for long enough.

Try adding a pinch of oregano to add extra flavour. You can also add a little thyme to the onions while they are frying.

A tasty variation of this recipe can be made my cooking some crispy bacon and crumbling it into the mixture. You can try normal or smoked bacon.

If the garlic taste isn't for you try substituting dill instead.

Cheddar Fondue

Ingredients

8 oz cream cheese
¾ cup milk
1 cup shredded medium cheddar cheese
1 small onion

Method

Chop the onion and cut the cream cheese into cubes.

Put the cream cheese and milk into a saucepan and put it on a low heat on the hob. Stir the mixture as it heats until it is nice and smooth. Continue stirring as you add the cheddar cheese. Continue stirring and heating until everything melts and blends together. At this point add the chopped onion.

Dip chunks of rough cut rustic French bread into the cheddar fondue and enjoy. You can also serve it with warm crusty bread. Also try pretzels, mini sausages, and apple slices.

A different taste can be achieved by frying and caramelizing the chopped onion before adding it in the normal way to the fondue in the saucepan.

You can try adding a clove of minced garlic for extra flavour especially if you like garlic.

For extra kick and heat add red pepper flakes and cayenne pepper.

You can make this into a nacho style dip by adding 2 jalapenos and a 1/3 cup of salsa.

Mushroom dip

Ingredients

4 oz can of mushrooms
2 tbsp butter
¼ tsp onion powder
Dash of hot pepper sauce
Pinch of freshly ground black pepper
¼ tsp nutmeg
¼ cup sour cream
3 oz cream cheese
1 tsp lemon juice
2 tbsp milk

Method

Drain the can of mushrooms and then coarsely blend them in a food processor or blender. Transfer the mushrooms to a frying pan and cook them in the butter on a medium heat for about a minute. Add the onion powder, hot pepper sauce and nutmeg to the mushrooms in the pan. Stir to combine the spices with the mushrooms.

Soften the cream cheese by putting it in the microwave for a few seconds. Put the cream cheese in a bowl and then stir in the sour cream, lemon juice and milk. Continue stirring until everything is well combined. Stir in the mushrooms from the pan and make sure that all of the ingredients are mixed well.

Serve the mushroom dip with potato chips or raw vegetables cut for dipping.

Thai style dip

Ingredients

¾ cup water
2 tsp cornstarch
1/3 cup seasoned rice vinegar
¼ cup brown sugar
1 ½ tbsp soy sauce
½ inch fresh ginger
2 cloves garlic
½ tsp crushed red pepper flakes
Chopped spring onions
Sesame seeds

Method

Grate the ginger and crush the garlic.

Put the water cornstarch, vinegar, brown sugar, soy sauce, grated ginger, garlic and pepper flakes into a small pan and whisk them together.

Put the saucepan on a medium heat and bring to the boil while continuing to whisk. Once the sauce has thickened take it from the heat and leave it to cool. Sprinkle chopped spring onions and sesame seeds on the top of the dip as a garnish before serving.

This is an ideal dip for spring rolls, egg rolls, chicken skewers and chicken strips in batter. It also goes well with cold shrimp and crab claws.

To make the sauce thicker simply increase the amount of cornstarch that you add.

Beef chilli cheese dip

Ingredients

1 pound lean ground beef
½ cup chopped green onion
½ cup chopped green bell pepper
¼ cup roasted red bell pepper
8 oz can tomato sauce
4 oz can of chopped mild green chillies
1 tbsp Worcestershire sauce
1 pound processed cheese spread
½ teaspoon cayenne pepper
½ teaspoon paprika

Method

Cut the processed cheese spread into cubes.

Put the ground beef in a pan on a medium heat and cook it until it is nicely browned. Drain off the fat and liquids from the beef and then add the green onion, green pepper, roasted red pepper, tomato sauce, chillies, Worcestershire sauce, cheese, paprika and cayenne.

Stir to combine the ingredients and then heat to boiling. Reduce the heat and simmer the mixture, while stirring it every now and then, for half an hour.

Serve the dip warm with corn chips or tacos.

Chicken Enchilada Dip

Ingredients

3 skinless chicken breast halves
16 oz light cream cheese
4 green onions
10 oz can of diced tomatoes with green chilli peppers
1 tsp minced garlic
1 tsp chopped coriander leaves
1 tsp chilli powder
1 tsp cumin powder
1 tsp dried oregano
1 tsp paprika

Method

Season the chicken breasts and then grill them until they are well cooked and then allow them to cool. Shred the cold chicken in a food processor.

Chop the green onions. Soften the cheese by putting it in the microwave for a few seconds on full power.

Drain off the liquid from the can of tomatoes and green chilli peppers and put to one side for use later.

Put the cream cheese, garlic, coriander leaves, chilli powder, cumin, oregano and paprika into a bowl and beat to combine and produce a smooth consistency. Next add the shredded chicken, green onions, diced tomatoes and green chilli peppers. Stir the ingredients to mix them and produce a smooth well combined dip. If the dip is too thick add the tomato juices, kept from draining the can earlier, a little at a time as you stir it until you get the right consistency.

Cover the bowl and place in the refrigerator to chill for 2 to 3 hour before serving.

This dip goes well with hard corn tortilla chips and soft flour tortillas.

For extra presentation and taste points you can top the chicken dip mixture in the serving dish with shredded cheddar cheese, fresh coriander leaves, fresh diced tomatoes, chopped green onions and sliced black olives.

You can spice up the recipe by adding hot pepper sauce and minced pickled jalapeno peppers.

If you are stuck for time you can use about 19 oz of drained canned chicken breast meat instead having to spend time grilling the raw chicken breasts.

You can make this into a hot dip by putting it in a baking dish and cooking it in a preheated oven set to 180C for about 15 minutes.

Mexican style hot bean dip

This is a great family dip and makes a huge amount so that you won't run out. It is good for kids but you can easily increase the heat by adding extra pepper sauce or green chillies or both!

Ingredients

8 oz cream cheese
1 cup sour cream
24 oz of canned refried beans
1 oz taco seasoning mix
6 drops hot pepper sauce
2 tbsp dried parsley
¼ cup chopped green onions
8 oz shredded Cheddar cheese
8 oz shredded Pepper Jack cheese

Method

Soften the cream cheese by heating it for a few seconds in the microwave.

Mix the cream cheese, sour cream and taco seasoning together in a bowl until they are well blended. Stir in the refried beans, parsley, green onions, hot pepper sauce, half of the cheddar cheese and half of the Pepper Jack cheese. Make sure that all of the ingredients are well combined.

Spoon the mixture into a suitable baking dish and sprinkle the top with the remaining Pepper Jack cheese and cheddar cheese. Put the dish into a preheated oven set to 180C and cook for about 20 minutes. Remove the dish when the cheese is browned a little. Serve while hot with tortilla chips.

If you want some extra kick in this recipe then you can add 2 cans of green chillies and some cayenne pepper. This way you can make it as fiery as you like.

Crab and spinach dip

Ingredients

10 oz frozen chopped spinach
1 six oz can crabmeat
8 oz cream cheese
1 cup plain yogurt
½ cup grated Parmesan cheese
½ cup light mayonnaise
2 garlic cloves
1 tsp crushed red pepper flakes
¼ tsp salt
¼ tsp pepper

Method

Thaw out the spinach and then squeeze it dry. Cut the cream cheese into cubes. Mince the garlic. Open the can of crab meat and drain off the liquid.

Combine the spinach, cream cheese, yogurt, Parmesan, mayonnaise, garlic, red pepper flakes, salt and pepper in a large pan. Heat the mixture over a low heat while stirring. Cook until the cream cheese cubes have melted. Stir in the crab and continue to cook until the dip is heated through. Don't boil the mixture.

Put the crab and spinach dip into a serving bowl. This dip goes well with crackers or baked tortilla chips.

Baked spinach and artichoke Dip

Ingredients

½ cup chopped green onions
2 tbsp butter
4 oz softened cream cheese
20 oz frozen creamed spinach
14 oz can artichoke hearts
4 oz mild Cheddar cheese
4 oz Swiss cheese
1 tbsp Worcestershire sauce
½ tsp Cajun seasoning
½ tsp minced fresh thyme
½ tsp hot pepper sauce
1 minced garlic clove
¼ cup grated Parmesan cheese

Method

Thaw out the spinach. Drain the liquid from the artichoke hearts and then rinse them in fresh cold water before chopping them. Shred the cheddar and Swiss cheeses.

Use a small frying pan to cook the green onions on a medium heat until they are tender. Put these to one side for use later. Put the cream cheese into a large bowl and then beat it until it has a smooth consistency. Mix in the cooked onions, spinach, artichoke hearts, Worcestershire sauce, Cajun seasoning, thyme, hot pepper sauce, garlic, cheddar and Swiss cheeses.

Put the mixture into a suitable sized baking dish and then place it into a preheated oven set at 180C for about 30 minutes. Top the mixture with the Parmesan cheese and then return to the oven until the cheese on top turns a nice golden colour.

Serve the dip while it is hot with pita chips or slices of crusty rustic bread

You can also try adding sun dried tomatoes to the recipe as a variation that has a greater sharpness and fresh taste.

Clam and cheese dip

Ingredients

3 six and half oz cans of minced clams
2 tbsp fresh lemon juice
¼ cup chopped onion
½ cup butter
1 pinch ground black pepper
1 cup dry Italian style bread crumbs
Extra virgin olive oil
8 oz shredded sharp Cheddar cheese

Method

Fry the onion in a pan with a little of the butter until they are browned.

Put the clams including juices, browned onion, lemon juice, butter, pepper and bread crumbs into a medium sized bowl and then drizzle with the olive oil. Mix the ingredients together and stir until they are well combined.

Spoon the mixture into a suitably sized baking dish and top with the shredded cheddar cheese. Bake in a preheated oven set at 180C for about 20 minutes. The dip is cooked once it is bubbling in the dish.

Serve the dip warm with crackers. It can also be served with celery sticks and carrots.

Mexican style layer dip

Ingredients

16 oz cream cheese
8 oz sour cream
1 dash hot pepper sauce
1 dash soy sauce
2 tsp lemon juice
16 oz jar salsa
1 bunch green onions
2 oz can of sliced black olives
½ head iceberg lettuce
8 oz finely shredded Cheddar cheese
1 large red pepper

Method

Soften the cream cheese by putting in the microwave for about 15 seconds. Chop the green onions. Rinse the lettuce and then drain and dry it before shredding it. Chop the red pepper.

Combine together the cream cheese, sour cream, lemon juice, hot sauce and soy sauce in a mixing bowl. Keep mixing until a creamy smooth consistency is produced. Spoon this mixture into a rectangular glass dish and spread it out into an even base layer for the dip.

Create a layer of salsa followed by layers of green onions, olives, shredded lettuce, cheddar cheese and red pepper over the base layer of cream cheese. Cover the top layer with cling film and then carefully press the layers of ingredients down to make them more compact. Put the dish into the refrigerator and chill before serving.

This dip goes well with tortilla chips especially if you get the scoop shaped ones.

To produce a spicier dip with more kick you can increase the amount of hot pepper sauce that you add. You can also choose a hotter salsa to use. More flavour can be achieved if you substitute a packet of taco seasoning for the hot pepper sauce and the soy sauce.

Reduced fat cream cheese and sour cream can be used in order to reduce the calories.

Conclusion

Experimentation is the name of the game. Once you get started with making dips you will see that there are plenty of variations that can be made. Some of these variations will produce interesting dips that you can add to your repertoire. You can try different herbs and different flavoured cheeses to start off with.

Dips are the ideal food to take to parties because they are easy to whip up and are always very popular with the guests because people like to eat nibbles when they are busy socializing. Looking at it this way a good dip could really make a party special!

Hot dips can also be eaten cold the next day and so there is no need for leftovers to be thrown away. They often have a subtly different flavour when cold, which adds an extra dimension to these types of dips. Another use for leftover dips is to use them as a sauce with a meal the next day. As a result a dip that goes well with chicken tenders could be used as a sauce with grilled or fried chicken the next day.

About the Author

Elisabetta Parisi has written several other Kindle and paperback books specializing in various recipes from different European countries including her home country Italy. Here are the details of some of the other books that you can buy.

Homemade Pasta Dough

How to make pasta dough for the best pasta dough recipe including pasta dough for ravioli and other fresh pasta dough recipe ideas

Elisabetta Parisi

http://www.amazon.com/Homemade-Pasta-Dough-including-ravioli/dp/147823458X/

Making your own pasta is a very satisfying way to spend your time in the kitchen. The rewards come from both the effort that you put in and the fantastic new tastes that you can create for your family and friends at meal time.

Homemade Pasta Dough explains how to make many different kinds of pasta from the raw ingredients. The book explains how to make pasta dough both by hand and using various machines to help cut down the work involved.

Fresh pasta made at home is a very healthy option and there are lots of ways that you can vary the pasta dough you make. This will then add life to your pasta meals. The book contains details of mixing, rolling, cutting, stuffing and shaping your pasta.

This is an updated and extended version of the original popular book with lots of new pasta dough recipes which will extend your pasta repertoire. There are also more details on stuffed pastas such as ravioli and tortellini as well as dessert style pasta. Also now included, are example recipes showing where the different pasta doughs and shapes can be used.

Tapas Recipes

Covers what are tapas and includes Spanish tapas recipes to make lots of tapas dishes so that you can build your own tapas menu based on Spanish tapas and other world tapas ideas

Elisabetta Parisi

http://www.amazon.com/Tapas-Recipes-Spanish-recipes-ebook/dp/B005KLTCEY/

Tapas Recipes has lots of tasty tapas foods for you to make at home. Tapas food is becoming more popular all of the time with tapas bars opening up across the world and big supermarkets stocking their own tapas lines. You can make your own tapas out of fresh ingredients, enjoy them with some Spanish wine and relive those glorious summer holiday times. Tapas are great as snacks and even better with wine or beer. They are also a great alternative to the usual sausage rolls and paste sandwiches of a typical buffet spread. Enjoy them on your own and contemplate the world or entertain with them it is your choice! Each recipe is easy to follow with no strange ingredients that are hard to get. Go on, have a change and make some tapas.

http://www.amazon.com/Panini-Recipes-sandwich-including-ebook/dp/B005F5GPHM

Panini Recipes can be exciting as well as quick. You are really missing out if you don't have this Italian inspired food at home. You can put just about anything into a panini so long as it is cooked first. The taste of a panini is influenced by the quality of the bread that you use. You can buy Italian bread but why not go that extra step and make some yourself. This book contains some easy recipes for panini bread including Ciabatta and Focaccia. You can make these quickly and improve your panini experience greatly. Try your new homemade panini bread with some of the exciting panini recipes in this book.

Penne Pasta Recipes

Penne pasta includes the popular recipes of Penne alla vodka, Penne arrabiata, Penne carbonara and baked Penne

Elisabetta Parisi

http://www.amazon.com/Penne-Pasta-Recipes-arrabiata-ebook/dp/B005JL4PWE/

Penne Pasta Recipes for great meals using this very versatile pasta shape. Penne is fantastic with sauces, in soups and with salads. Learn how to cook Penne so that it can absorb and hold the sauces you add to it. Make the basic Marinara sauce and you can use this as the basis for a lot of other recipes and build upon its flavors to produce many exciting dishes including Penne alla Vodka and Penne Carbonara. Feel the spice in Penne Arrabiatta and cook with Italian sausage for extra flavor. Learn the recipes in this book and you will be able to produce a huge variety of pasta dishes rather than the inevitable Spag Bol which seems to turn up on the menu every week.

32635436R00051

Printed in Poland
by Amazon Fulfillment
Poland Sp. z o.o., Wrocław